MW01630357

Introduction

In 2019, the whole world was affected by a virus called COVID-19. To keep everyone healthy and safe, many stores, restaurants, and school buildings closed. For the first time, people were asked to wear masks over their nose and mouth when they left their homes. These masks were different, and they caused some BIG feelings. Some people felt sad. Some people felt scared. Some people felt lonely. And some people missed seeing smiles. These feelings were all normal. It is OK to feel sad; it is OK to feel scared; it is OK to feel lonely, and it is OK to miss smiles.

This is a very special book. It is written to honor all the helpers you meet at school. It is also written to help you feel a little more comfortable when you see your favorite helpers in their masks. Lastly, it is written so you can remember that behind each mask is a big, loving smile!

This book is dedicated to my smiles:
Danny, Carter, & Sophia

"GOOD MORNING!"

As the big yellow bus drives up to my house, I see Mr. Mark. He is my bus driver. Mr. Mark is funny and kind. He dresses up on Halloween and gives out treats on Valentine's Day. Mr. Mark picks me up on time every morning and welcomes me with a cheerful,

"GOOD MORNING! TODAY IS GOING TO BE A GREAT DAY!"

Mr. Mark wears a green mask. It has little yellow splats on it and it covers his nose and mouth. I know that behind Mr. Mark's mask is a big, happy smile.

SCHOOL BUS
STOP

"LOOK BOTH WAYS!"

When the bus drops me off at school, I am greeted by Mrs. Jackson. She is our crossing guard. Mrs. Jackson is always singing. She loves to dance too. Every morning, Mrs. Jackson holds up her red stop sign so I can safely cross the parking lot at school. When I cross, Mrs. Jackson stops singing, just for a moment, to say,

"LOOK BOTH WAYS BEFORE YOU CROSS!"

Mrs. Jackson wears a purple mask with a pink rabbit's nose sewn on to it. The mask covers her nose and mouth. I know that behind Mrs. Jackson's mask is a giant, happy smile.

STOP

"GOOD MORNING CLASS!"

My teacher's name is Mr. Smith. He is kind and patient. Mr. Smith never gets mad, even when we accidently forget to finish our work. Every morning we sit criss-cross applesauce in a circle on the big checkered rug in the front of our classroom. Mr. Smith sits with us in in the circle in his squeaky rocking chair and talks about the weather, our lunch menu, and the specials for the day. Mr. Smith always starts the same way,

"GOOD MORNING CLASS! I AM SO HAPPY TO SEE YOU AND SHARE OUR DAY TOGETHER."

Mr. Smith wears a mask that looks just like a zebra. It has black and white stripes and purple straps that attach to his ears. Mr. Smith also wears glasses and sometimes when he laughs, they get all foggy. It looks really silly! I know that behind Mr. Smith's mask is a ginormous, happy smile.

"I PLEDGE ALLEGIANCE..."

Every day after circle, we turn on the morning show to see our principal, Mrs. Reyes. She is the leader of our school. Mrs. Reyes announces every student's name on their birthday, and teachers too! She really likes birthdays! Mrs. Reyes also guides us through the Pledge of Allegiance. She stands up, puts her hand on her heart, and says,

"LET'S ALL SAY TOGETHER, I PLEDGE ALLEGIANCE TO THE FLAG...."

Mrs. Reyes wears a red and blue mask over her nose and mouth. Red and blue are our school colors. I bet she even has a mask with a tiny picture of our school mascot, a tiger. Mrs. Reyes has a lot of school spirit! I know that behind her mask is a super enthusiastic, ready-to-start-the-day-smile!

PRINCIPAL

"DO YOU WANT DESSERT?"

My favorite part of the school day is lunch. We eat in the cafeteria and then we get to go outside to play. Miss Jones is our lunch monitor. She always gives me extra ice cream because she knows how much I love ice cream. I make sure to say thank you when I go through the lunch line because Miss Jones always winks at me when she says,

"DO YOU WANT DESSERT TODAY?"

Miss Jones wears a mask with a big cheeseburger on it.
I think it is the perfect mask for a lunch monitor, especially Miss Jones, because she is so kind. I know that behind her mask is a huge, friendly smile.

"TIME TO GO HOME!"

On the bus ride home, I look out the window and see lots of helpers. First, I see our police officer helping kids cross the street. His name is Officer Jon. He tells lots of jokes and makes sure we are safe at school. Officer Jon has a football mask covering his nose and mouth. It is his favorite sport!

As we drive by the fire department, I see three firemen shining up their trucks with a big yellow cloth. They wave as we drive by and I notice that they all have the same mask covering their noses and mouths. The masks are dark blue with red stars and the stars match the color of their firetrucks.

As we drive by my doctor's office, I see Dr. Frank and Nurse Olivia. I wave to them from my bus and they see me and wave back. Dr. Frank and Nurse Olivia are so nice. They always make me feel safe, even when I get a shot, and they let me pick a treat after my appointments. Dr. Frank's mask looks like a dinosaur and Nurse Olivia's mask is gold with tiny black music notes. I bet she plays the piano!

As we pull on to my street, I see Jeff, our mailman. Jeff is the best! He always has a treat for my dog, Ginger. Jeff is busily delivering packages to the houses on my street. He is wearing a mask with an envelope on it. Jeff really loves his job as a mailman!

The police officer, the firemen, Dr. Frank, Nurse Olivia and Jeff the mailman all wear their masks to be safe. I know that behind each of their masks is a great big, goofy smile.

MAIL

"I MISSED YOU!"

Every day after school, my papa picks me up from the bus stop. Papa drives a super cool silver truck that is so high off the ground, I need a special step to climb inside. Papa is the nicest person I know. He makes me snacks after school and helps me start my homework. Papa tells me stories about his adventures and always lets me pick which show we watch on tv together. Every day when I get in his truck, Papa says,

"I MISSED YOU TODAY WHILE YOU WERE AT SCHOOL.
I CAN'T WAIT TO HEAR ALL ABOUT YOUR DAY!"

It is important for my papa to wear a mask. He has one for each day of the week. Today he is wearing my favorite. It is a mask with a monkey on it. Monkeys are my favorite animals. I know that behind Papa's mask is the most loving smile you have ever seen!

MY FAMILY.

After a fun day at school, I love to hang out with my family. We go to the park. We go on bike rides and play games together. Tonight, we are going on a hike but first we stop at the grocery store for snacks. We all wear our masks in the store. My mask is yellow with orange stripes. My brother's mask is green with soccer balls on it and my sister's mask is navy blue, because that is her favorite color. My mom and dad wear masks too. My mom's mask is pink with purple dots and my dad's mask has a palm tree on it, because he loves the beach.

We wear our masks to the store to stay safe and healthy. We know that behind our masks are our super happy, super silly, super loving, gigantic smiles.

About the Author

Dr. Hennessey Lustica, PhD, LMHC is the proud mom of three amazing children, Danny, Carter, and Sophia. Hennessey's husband Dan is a high school Math teacher in Western New York. Together, they love to travel (especially to tropical locations), eat delicious food, and hang out with family and friends. Hennessey and Dan are both dedicated educators with 20 years of experience working with students and families. Hennessey has spent the greater part of her career as a School Counselor, which she considers to be the most challenging and rewarding job in the world. She is also licensed as a Mental Health Counselor in New York State, where she works with children, adolescents, and families experiencing anxiety, trauma, and depression. She has published works on school-based mental health and presented regionally and nationally on all things school counseling related. Hennessey currently holds two positions, Community Schools Mental Health Grant Director and Assistant Professor in the Clinical Mental Health Counseling program at Medaille College.

About the Illustrator

Fred Sovie is the proud dad of two daughters, Annabelle and Aliza. Fred's wife Becky is a Kindergarten teacher in Upstate New York. Fred has 29 years of experience as a middle and high school art teacher. When he is not drawing, Fred enjoys exercising, teaching, and spending time with his family.

Made in the USA
Monee, IL
20 August 2020

38806378R00017